HOW CIVILITY WORKS

HOW CIVILITY WORKS

KEITH J. BYBEE

stanford briefs
An Imprint of Stanford University Press
Stanford, California

Stanford University Press
Stanford, California

Printed in the United States of America
on acid-free, archival-quality paper

Library of Congress Cataloging-in-Publication Data

Names: Bybee, Keith J., 1965- author.
Title: How civility works / Keith J. Bybee.
Description: Stanford, California : Stanford Briefs, an imprint of
   Stanford University Press, 2016. | Includes bibliographical
   references.
Identifiers: LCCN 2016030148| ISBN 9781503601543 (pbk. : alk.
   paper) | ISBN 9781503601826 (electronic)
Subjects: LCSH: Courtesy—Political aspects—United States. |
   Political culture—United States. | Freedom of expression—United
   States. | United States—Politics and government.
Classification: LCC JK1726 .B93 2016 | DDC 306.20973—dc23
LC record available at https://lccn.loc.gov/2016030148

Typeset by Classic Typography in 11/15 Adobe Garamond

CONTENTS

1 The Promise of Civility   1

2 Civility Defined   7

3 The Excellence of Free Expression   25

4 Are You Just Being Polite?   43

5 Strength in Weakness   67

Sources and Further Reading   71

Acknowledgments   79

HOW CIVILITY WORKS

1 THE PROMISE OF CIVILITY

Can we all get along?

In 1992 Rodney King plaintively posed this question in front of television news cameras after the police officers who had beaten him were acquitted and the streets of Los Angeles erupted in riots. The rampage lasted five days and in the end left over sixty people dead and one thousand buildings destroyed. King's plea did not stop the rioting, but he did achieve a kind of fame, and the call for peaceful coexistence would follow him for the rest of his life. When he died, "Can We All Get Along" was placed on his tombstone.

King spoke during a time of intense violence, but his question has a far broader resonance and can be asked of American society as a whole. We regularly experience episodes of turbulent protest. And beyond any particular instance of turmoil, we inhabit and sustain a contentious public culture. Our politics are preoccupied with the demonization of opponents. Our news media is saturated with aggressive bluster and vitriol. Our workplaces are rife with boorish behavior. Our digital platforms teem with expressions of disrespect and invective. Reflecting these conditions, surveys show that a significant majority of Americans believe we are living in an age of unusual anger and discord. A quarter of a century after King wondered whether we can get along, we find ourselves in a social world filled with conflict and hostility.

A host of authors and observers have diagnosed our malaise as a lack of civility and prescribed civility's return as the cure. Americans once treated one another with far greater respect and consideration, the argument goes. If we can recover the traditionally courteous modes of relating to one another, we will find that our public life can be more restrained and peaceful. Political disagreements will remain, but new compromises will become possible as adversaries turn their attention away from maligning one another's character and focus instead on scrutinizing competing policies. The news media will model civil engagement in its coverage, emphasizing fact-based analysis rather than sensationalizing conflict and relentlessly stoking animosities. Everyday exchanges between individuals—including those on social media, in website comment sections, and at work—will become more sociable, with substantially less tolerance for harassment and insult.

IS CIVILITY POSSIBLE OR DESIRABLE?

Many say that civility is quite important. But the standard argument for it rests on shaky foundations. To begin with, it is not clear how we can rely on a settled store of past courtesies to save us when there is in fact no period in the past when civility was fully established and secure from challenge.

It is true that many people today feel that civility has vanished, and true that the cause can be traced to contemporary factors like political polarization and the rise of the internet. Yet it is also true, as historians of civility have noted, that generations of Americans have felt threatened by escalating incivility and they had no trouble finding causes in their own time. At different points during the twentieth century, Americans chalked up the deterioration of public conduct to jazz music, World War I, the Great Depression, World War II, the Vietnam War, the Civil Rights Movement, rock and roll, and the large-scale entry of women into the workforce. Nineteenth-century Americans blamed the Civil War, new immigrants, urban life, the vulgar rich, and the insolent poor. Talk of social crisis and fear of coarsening relations were also easy to find in the eighteenth century. James Madison along with many of our Founders complained about the truculence and crass materialism produced by the grasping, interest-ridden politics in the states. Given such a long history of rudeness, why should we believe that people are capable of getting along now?

In addition to this question of capacity there is also a question of motivation. The standard argument for civility begins with the assumption that our current ways of interacting are obviously dysfunctional and in need of repair. Yet instead of stipulating that we have failed, one could argue that our contentious public culture is a genuine accomplishment that we should wish to preserve.

For much of the modern era the courts have broadly interpreted the guarantees of the First Amendment. The result, as the Supreme Court noted in its landmark decision *New York Times v. Sullivan*, is that our public discussion has intentionally been kept "uninhibited, robust, and wide-open." Caustic critique, furious rants, and outright lies go largely unchecked by the Constitution to ensure that the greatest possible diversity of claims floods into the public sphere. Some views may seem too abrasive and offensive to endure. But as Justice Holmes observed almost one hundred years ago, "when men have realized that time has upset many fighting faiths, they may come to believe, even more than they believe the very foundations of their own conduct, that the ultimate good desired is better reached by free trade in ideas—that the best test of truth is the power of the thought to get itself accepted in the competition of the market, and that truth is the only ground upon which their wishes safely can be carried out." Nor does the value of untrammeled opinion stop with the discovery of truth and the exposure of injustice. Liberty of expression also allows for expansive breadth of thought and an extraordinary range for self-definition. Both of these things are very valuable. Indeed, according to Justice Brandeis, the development of conditions necessary to "make men free to develop their faculties" is nothing less than the final goal of government.

In short, our free speech society provides many advantages and in return asks only that we speak our minds and have thick skins. Why should we seek a more genteel means of managing our behavior?

The question of whether we are able to be civil, as well as the question of why we should want to be civil, can be answered by examining how civility works. The following pages are devoted to such an examination. As we shall see, there is substantial disagreement over what should count as civil behavior; strong criticism of civility's repressive regimentation; and serious concern about civility's authenticity. These disagreements and criticisms are themselves tied to underlying conditions, including the heterogeneity and dynamism of American society, a robust tradition of free expression, and our frequent inability to live up to our collective ideals.

Although my examination will turn up reasons to doubt civility and to worry about the endless proliferation of conflict, I will argue that the deeper, incongruous truth is that civility's strengths are ultimately in its weaknesses. The very features that make civility ineffective and undesirable also account for civility's power and appeal. Can we all get along? If we live by the paradoxes on which civility depends then yes, we can, and yes, we should.

What is civility? And how is it organized, enacted, and enforced? By taking up these questions, we can begin to understand why so many people have trouble getting along.

In the most general sense civility is a code of public conduct. It is not the only such code. Politeness and courtesy are readily recognized codes of public conduct. So too are chivalry and gallantry. All of these modes of behavioral management, including civility, are forms of good manners.

The different forms of manners cluster and blend in several ways, yet each also retains its own meaning. Chivalry, at its origins, referred to the piety and valor expected of medieval knights. Gallantry came along several centuries later and described the ideal behavior of aristocrats. The two sets of manners demand different actions: gallantry entails dashing deeds and ornate expressions of formal regard, while chivalry stresses self-sacrificing acts of kindness and protection. These different requirements frequently run together in contemporary discussions, and chivalry and gallantry are now often viewed as essentially equivalent practices primarily concerned with the treatment of women.

Unlike chivalry and gallantry, politeness is not narrowly preoccupied with the honor due women. On the contrary, polite society has rules that are meant to govern the behavior of everyone within it. This breadth of application is paired with an element of elevation: politeness is a refined set of good manners aligned with the interests and pursuits of high culture. Although people may sometimes refer to ordinary politeness, polite behavior generally carries an air of polish and urbane sophistication. Polite elegance is to be displayed with polite restraint. When taken to extremes of elaborate formality and pretension, politeness is branded as politesse, a disparaging term that is used to criticize a tendency to push refining impulses too far.

Like politeness, courtesy also has a link to elite affairs. Courtesy initially drew its name from princely courts and referred to the gracious behavior of courtly gentlemen. Unlike politeness, courtesy did not retain its patrician patina. Over time courtesy became less associated with courtiers and ultimately took on a more democratic cast. This more plebian descendant is now known as common courtesy and it signifies an everyday form of correct conduct.

Civility is a close cousin of both politeness and courtesy. As Norbert Elias documented in his massive two-volume series *The Civilizing Process*, civility emerged out of courtesy during the Middle Ages. Compared to its medieval predecessor, civility called for a more self-conscious molding of personal behavior to conform to norms of appropriateness and to facilitate coordination in increasingly complex urban communities. After being adopted by the upper classes (and connected with politeness), civility gradually spread throughout society, developing into a standard of conduct for all citizens in the polity. By the mid-1500s an understanding of civility as "behavior proper to the intercourse of civilized people" had been cemented in the English-speaking world.

The intersecting histories of civility, courtesy, and politeness—as well as the fact that all three codes now apply to broad swaths of society—lead many people to treat these schemes of manners as closely related. The family resemblance between these three forms is useful for conveying emphasis and orientation. For example, to underscore that being civil is a kind of cultural achievement, one can render civility as a kind of politeness. To highlight the everyday utility of being civil, one can relate the requirements of civility in the language of courtesy. Over the course of the argument here, it will occasionally be helpful to reference civility in terms of politeness or courtesy and to remind ourselves that the three varieties of manners overlap in important ways.

We can also speak directly about civility's own core meaning. Just as we can distinguish the polish of politeness from the daily devotions of common courtesy, we can find a distinctive significance in civility's foundational role. As the standard for all citizens, civility is the baseline of decent behavior and its requirements outline the most basic kinds of consideration that we owe one another in public life. We might frame civility's baseline function negatively as the bare minimum of good manners steering people away from only the most blatant rudeness. Alternatively and more positively, we might view civility as a threshold condition that precedes and permits the kinds of interaction required by the other codes of conduct. Either way, a sense of fundamentality is civility's central defining feature. And this central sense helps explain why the perceived decline of civility evokes a chorus of alarm. If civility is meant to be the zero point for appropriate behavior, then incivility undermines the rudiments of social order and all is lost.

AM I BEING RUDE?

How is one supposed to actually go about being well mannered? To be civil—just as to be chivalrous, gallant, polite, or courteous—is to follow the appropriate rules and requirements. These rules and requirements are generally known as etiquette or decorum, and their number and specificity varies substantially depending on the source consulted. As a teenager in colonial America, George Washington wrote out 110 precepts for his *Rules of Civility & Decent Behavior in Company & Conversation*, listing equal respect as the first commandment of civility ("Every Action done in Company, ought to be with Some Sign of Respect, to those that are Present") and ending with a directive to maintain moral sensibilities ("Labor to keep alive in your breast that little spark of celestial fire called conscience").

More recently, P. M. Forni, director of the Civility Initiative and author of *Choosing Civility*, has settled on twenty-five rules of civil etiquette, including "Speak kindly," "Refrain from idle complaints," and "Respect the environment and be gentle." Lynne Truss, an author who decries the collapse of civility in her book *Talk to the Hand*, boils down all manners to a single rule: "remember you are with other people; show some consideration." *Emily Post's Etiquette*, now in its eighteenth edition, not only lists a number of everyday manners, common courtesies, and guidelines for living but also details specific rules of behavior for dozens of different situations, ranging from dining and traveling, to work, weddings, funerals, and official life.

The variation in the range and domain of etiquette gives us our first clue to civility's precarious state. Which set of rules is one to follow? And how can one be sure that a selected body of rules is properly translated into concrete action? We might respond by noting that manners of all kinds are first learned at home, the rules of good behavior being handed down from parent to child. But this answer simply pushes the concern for uniformity back one level. How do we ensure that families are instilling the same precepts and teaching the same methods of application?

We would expect home schooling in civility to be consistent throughout a static, homogenous society. A society with a measure of dynamism and heterogeneity will produce more mixed results.

The United States has greatly transformed since its inception and it continues to change even now. We began with a traditional rank-ordered society inherited from England in the colonial era. Since then, our way of life has been repeatedly refashioned. The rise of mass markets and mass democracy, the abolition of slavery, the growth of cities, the influx of different waves of immigration, the accretion of vast government power, the social movement for civil rights, the reconfiguration of gender roles, the alterations in family formation, the explosion of digital communication, the increasing engagement with global politics and commerce—all of these factors (and more) have helped create a nation shot through with diversity and disagreement.

We should not be surprised to find that conceptions of civility have altered as conditions develop and change. American citizenship, Judith Shklar once observed, is "not a notion that can be discussed intelligibly in a static and empty social space." As forms of social organization and modes of relating to one another repeatedly shift, ideas about the behavior required in public life will continually transform. It is true that civility was, at its medieval origins, derived from the relatively fixed model of conduct employed in royal courts. But there is no longer a central model of appropriate conduct, and manners are democratically and flexibly fashioned from the assortment of different beliefs and practices found in modern society. Without an established rule of behavior handed down from an aristocracy, we employ many different methods to establish rules for ourselves.

Our views of civility today clearly reflect such diversity and ongoing ferment. As readers of advice columns well know, we have many different understandings of the basic consideration and signs of respect required in public life. Some manage to learn a common set of current courtesies, while others doggedly cling to the retrograde standards of conduct from bygone eras. Others have their own idiosyncratic rulebooks of etiquette, and many people insist that the only rule of good behavior is that each person be natural and authentic (the sole commandment of this latter code is "You do you"). Even those who share the same general conception of civility are often divided by uncertainty and quarrels about the actions best suited to specific contexts.

The multiple understandings of appropriate conduct make it easy for individuals to spot incivility when they experience it, but harder to identify incivility when they inflict it. We keenly feel the slight when someone has not shown us the respect we think we deserve. We are often less aware of how offensive our own deeds are to others who have different interpretations of required decorum. In their fourteen years of research on how people are treated in the workplace, Christine Porath and Christine Pearson found that 98 percent of those polled had experienced incivility on the job. At the same time, substantial numbers of employees and managers reported that they did not fully understand how to treat others civilly. And one quarter of those who offended their work colleagues had no idea they had been rude. We tend to take our own good manners for granted, as Henry Alford writes in *Would It Kill You to Stop Doing That?* and we tend to assume that our own comportment is always commendable. As for bad manners, we at once recognize their ubiquity and "almost never think that we ourselves have them."

Civility, like all forms of good manners, does have a way of discouraging bad behavior: individuals are obliged to police etiquette by watching for rudeness and chastising offenders. The first party to be monitored is oneself: the civil individual should be on the lookout to ensure she is conforming to the rules. Public shaming serves as backstop whenever individual self-supervision lapses.

Whether directed at oneself or others, reprimands can certainly be formidable means of influencing behavior. Judith Martin, the syndicated columnist and author who writes under the name Miss Manners, claims that her "look of disapproval has been known to sizzle bacon." And as Jon Ronson documents, the internet has amplified the power of public shaming in a variety of ways. Yet as powerful as such enforcement can be, it does not inevitably drive everyone to comply with a single standard. Self-policing binds people to whatever version of etiquette they already accept. Public finger wagging has a greater chance of moving everyone in the same direction, but its efficacy depends on targeted individuals accepting that they have done something blameworthy in the first place. When publicly admonished to behave, people already persuaded of their own propriety may perhaps pause to reflect on their actions and decide to change their behavior. Or they may shrug off the rebuke (or react with anger) and afterward continue to carry on just as they had before.

For the person witnessing plain rudeness or administering a disregarded reprimand, the offender's conduct is experienced as evidence of civility's demise. However, the underlying problem is often not the absence of civility but its excess. It is the profusion of different beliefs about correct behavior that creates an environment in which common courtesies do not seem very common.

COMPETING CODES OF CONDUCT

Friction between different notions of civility has existed throughout American history. During the late 1700s, as the historian Gordon Wood explains, the Federalist supporters of the new Constitution practiced a patrician-led politics organized around disinterestedness, the requirement that public officials unselfishly rise above all pecuniary interests in their lawmaking (we retain something of this original requirement today in our disdain for special interests). Against this established approach to the conduct of public life, the Anti-Federalists claimed that all of politics was a competition among interests and they refused to conform either their arguments or their actions to the etiquette of disinterestedness.

The Federalists reacted to this rejection of the traditional leadership ideal with disbelief and fury. Surely the

Anti-Federalists could not seriously maintain that no one, no matter how educated or virtuous, was capable of seeing beyond his own narrow concerns. To see self-interested action everywhere was to deny that any class of individuals was capable of pursuing the public good, and to push the American people, as Benjamin Rush put it, to the verge of "degenerating into savages or devouring each other like beasts of prey." Yet what the Federalists understood as a social crisis and a return to barbarism, the Anti-Federalists presented as the requisites of good order. Anti-Federalists like William Findley felt no sting from the Federalist rebukes. Findley argued that the cardinal rule of appropriate behavior was not to pretend some aristocratic class was entirely above parochial concerns, but rather to make sure that all claims of self-interest were treated with equal regard. In America, Findley insisted, "no man has a greater claim of special privilege for his £100,000 than I have for my £5."

Female political activists were embroiled in a different set of disputes over civility during the 1800s. As John Kasson notes in his account of nineteenth-century American manners, *Rudeness and Civility*, conventions of good behavior at the time required women to remain dependent on men as their guardians in public spaces. A woman appearing in the streets of town without a male escort invited opprobrium, and a woman standing alone, arguing against slavery or for the right to vote, was considered to be nothing short of indecent. "Contending for your rights stirs up the selfish feelings of others," one 1837 etiquette manual for women advised, "but a readiness to yield them awakes generous sentiments." Given these conditions, the political work of women could not be limited to giving speeches, lobbying policymakers, or proposing model legislation. It was also necessary to advocate a different conception of appropriate conduct that allowed women to participate in the public sphere as independent actors.

Conflict between different views of appropriate public behavior was also at the heart of the Civil Rights Movement in the twentieth century. Following the end of Reconstruction, a network of Jim Crow laws established formal racial segregation throughout the former Confederacy. These laws were surrounded and sustained by rules of racial etiquette that relegated African Americans to a subordinate position. Martin Luther King Jr. described what "proper" treatment of blacks looked like under these rules: "your first name becomes 'nigger,' your middle name becomes 'boy' (however old you are) and your last name becomes 'John,' and your wife and mother are never given the respected title of 'Mrs.'" King rejected this code of conduct and demanded that African Americans be shown the same signs of respect as whites. From the perspective of those steeped in the old racial etiquette, King's egalitarian demands were gross violations of good manners that were to be sharply criticized and quickly suppressed. King and other "outside agitators" were castigated for being ill mannered and for refusing to keep to their appropriate station in the racial order.

Rival visions of proper conduct continue to roil public life today. During the 2016 presidential election cycle,

Republican candidate Donald Trump began the primary season by calling many Mexican immigrants rapists, by pointedly questioning the intelligence of one of his opponents, and by condemning the esteemed veteran John McCain for having been a prisoner of war. For many, Trump's comments went beyond the ordinary boundaries of appropriate electioneering—boundaries that as Stephen Hess notes in *The Little Book of Campaign Etiquette* already allow for plenty of criticism and confrontation. Outraged observers called on Trump to apologize for his broad slander and personal attacks. The *Wall Street Journal* editorial board declared that Trump had arrived at his "inevitable self-immolation." Rather than retreat, Trump doubled down. He dismissed the *Wall Street Journal* ("Who cares!"), labeled his critics "total losers," and insinuated that tough questioning he received at a candidate debate occurred because one of the moderators was menstruating. Trump then called for the United States and Mexico to be separated by a massive wall, and he demanded that all Muslims be temporarily banned from entering the country.

Trump is a notorious self-promoter and it may seem like a stretch to put his antics in the same league as historic disagreements over appropriate public conduct. Rather than crediting Trump with an alternative understanding of civility, why not just say that his brazen rudeness was a stunt designed to enhance his own celebrity and feed his desire for importance? After all, as Susan Herbst observes in her book *Rude Democracy*, etiquette violation can be a tactic that political actors use to achieve their objectives. It could be that Trump counted on the existence of some consensus beliefs about the appropriate limits of polite politicking. He then intentionally provoked a defense of the consensus in hopes of triggering an avalanche of publicity.

Such self-serving moves are infuriating, but they do not present a different vision of what civility should be. The strategic offender challenges reigning civilities with spectacular breaches of decorum. On a deeper level, however, the strategic offender actually affirms prevailing forms of good manners by relying on their acceptance. Strategic incivility performs a kind of jujitsu, seizing the indignation generated to protect civility and redirecting it to serve personal purposes. The breach of good manners is real; even so, the impact on the larger practice of civility is usually localized, and the strategic offender attempts to use the existing order, not to displace it.

The benefits of provocation no doubt accounted for some of Trump's personal motivations and success. But strategic incivility does not fully explain why he won enthusiastic praise from voters for "telling it like it is." Trump—like eighteenth-century Anti-Federalists, nineteenth-century female abolitionists and suffragettes, and twentieth-century civil rights activists—also offered a new code of public conduct. Although Trump could be seen as an extraordinary opportunist or a vulgar bully, his supporters saw an independent iconoclast with no patience for the equal measure of consideration that "political correctness" bestowed on a diverse array of groups. In place of political correctness Trump advanced a recalibrated scale of respect that better suited those who disliked and distrusted the conventional pieties of public discourse. This recalibration produced inflammatory insults and it also resulted in praise and the possibility of due regard for deserving people who had been lumped together with the unworthy. "When Mexico sends its people, they're not sending their best," Trump told his supporters. "They're not sending you." Decent Mexican immigrants, as well as decent Muslims and good women, could be found. Such decency and goodness should not, however, be presumed simply to avoid giving offense. Trump's new brand of civility promised that the wheat could be separated from the chaff.

LAW AS AN ALTERNATIVE TO CIVILITY?

Civility is a foundational form of good manners that is understood and implemented in a variety of conflicting ways. We are all in fact capable of being civil—but not always on the same terms nor in the same fashion. Quite frequently one person violates another's understanding of appropriate conduct. And it is not uncommon for reprobates to stubbornly continue offending after they have been shown the error of their ways. Some of these boorish behaviors may be traced to self-interested actors who deliberately commit incivilities for the sake of personal advancement. Yet in many instances, including past and present political conflicts, rudeness results because competing conceptions of correct conduct are in play. "Rather than there being no manners," Henry Hitchings writes in his book-length investigation of English and American manners, "there are multitudes of conflicting manners, fraught with ambiguity." So long as our society remains dynamic and diverse, the contention between different notions of civility will persist. As a consequence each of us should expect to feel at one point or another that shamelessness is rampant and decency is under existential threat.

In reaction to such discomfiting circumstances, one may be tempted to enlist formal authority. If rudeness cannot be brought under control by cajoling and admonishments, then maybe public ordinances, regulation, or lawsuits will do the trick. It is just this sort of thinking that has periodically led to official codes prohibiting incivilities like offensive speech and indecent films.

Law appeals as a solution in part because it has much stronger sanctions than civility. Backed by state power, law can more effectively induce compliance by mandating behavior and imposing stiff penalties. Unlike civility, which comes in a cacophony of different rules and interpretations, law has the authority to call a single tune and to make sure that everyone marches in time. As Miss Manners herself has observed, law "can compel where Miss Manners can only wheedle."

Along with its connection to coercive power, law has the advantage of being arranged as a true system of rules rather than as a mere set (as is the case with civility and all other forms of manners). The body of law not only features primary rules that directly control individual conduct, but also contains secondary rules that order and manage the primary rules. The secondary legal rules establish institutions and processes that specify how other legal rules are to be recognized as authoritative, how legal rules are to be updated, how legal rules are to be applied, and how legal rules are to be adjudicated in cases of dispute. These secondary rules are a crucial feature of law and are essential for producing stable and efficient order. Indeed, the great legal philosopher H.L.A. Hart considered the creation of secondary rules to be as significant for human development as the invention of the wheel. Civility by contrast is entirely without any secondary level of governing rules and is missing the regulative institutions that such rules create. There is no official procedure or entity that authoritatively tells us how proper etiquette is to be known, applied, or amended across the whole of society. With the organizational resources that civility lacks, law is able to do a far better job of securing agreement on the rules everyone is required to obey.

In spite of its clear benefits, law's formal authority is a temptation worth resisting. The clash of conflicting civilities is often unsettling, and many people understandably long for a society in which everyone adheres to a single standard of appropriate public behavior. Yet when we enlist legal force we usually make matters worse by greatly raising the stakes in daily disputes over how people ought to behave. Moreover to give in to the desire for legal uniformity is to ignore the deep diversity and dynamic change that give rise to a welter of different manners in the first place. To seek legal uniformity is also to embrace the mistaken belief that civility can only thrive when there is clear consensus on what the terms of appropriate conduct are. It is true that civility is often thought to be in crisis. But as we shall see, the crisis grows directly out of that which makes our attachment to civility robust and enduring.

3 THE EXCELLENCE OF FREE EXPRESSION

It can be quite aggravating when we fail to arrive at universally shared standards of appropriate public behavior. Nonetheless, history is full of conflicts between competing codes of conduct. We seem to generate continual frustration by repeatedly falling short of agreement on the basic kinds of consideration required in public life.

Is this really a problem? Rather than seeking consensus on civility, many have argued that people should be allowed to present themselves more or less as they like. The themes of uninhibited expression and unfettered self-definition run throughout the modern Supreme Court's interpretation of the First Amendment. And the roots of this argument run even deeper than current legal doctrine. In the middle of the 1800s, more than a half century before the Supreme Court began actively championing First Amendment rights, the classic case for broad personal freedom was powerfully developed in John Stuart Mill's essay *On Liberty*.

According to Mill, it is very often the case that conflicting opinions each possess some grain of truth. In such situations progress toward the whole truth can be made only through the free competition of ideas, a competition that Mill called "the rough process of a struggle between combatants fighting under hostile banners." The ardent advocates participating in the competition of ideas are themselves unlikely to gain a better or more accurate understanding of issues. If anything, advocates tend to become more sectarian, inflexible, and extreme during heated disputes with their opponents. It is the audience, "the calmer and more disinterested bystander," that benefits from no-holds-barred argument. By attending to the freewheeling opinions of fervent dissenters and impassioned partisans, the audience identifies error, learns new truths, and gains a more vital grasp of the truths it already knows to be sound. The "truth has no chance," Mill wrote, "but in proportion as every side of it, every opinion which embodies any fraction of the truth, not only finds advocates, but is so advocated as to be listened to."

Free expression not only allows whole truths to rise and flourish but also permits individuals to follow the widest range of life plans. Liberty of action and freedom to fashion one's own identity are essential goods, and necessary for human excellence. "Human nature is not a machine to be built after a model, and set to do exactly the work prescribed for it," Mill argued. Human nature is instead "a tree, which requires itself to grow and develop itself on all sides, according to the tendency of the inward forces which make it a living thing."

Great personal freedom not only yields important benefits without requiring agreement on a code of civil conduct; insistence on a shared code may actually preclude the progressive discovery of truth and the ongoing development of human faculties that personal freedom promises. Systems of manners can be used to shore up hierarchies in the community, drawing distinctions between courteous and rude behavior in ways that entrench a pecking order across classes. When deployed in this fashion, civility becomes an impediment to change, insulating dominant groups from challenge and suppressing free competition of ideas along with experiments in living.

There is in fact a long history of defending good manners on the grounds that they protect an inegalitarian order. Consider *Hints on Etiquette and the Usages of Society with a Glance at Bad Habits*, written by Charles William Day and published in 1834. Day's book attracted a huge readership: in its first twenty years alone, *Hints on Etiquette* ran through twenty-eight editions in England and America. Day understood that egalitarian sensibilities were on the rise, but he thought equality had no place in the world of decorum. He advised that shopkeepers and tradespeople "will do well to remember that people are respectable in their own sphere only, and when they attempt to step out of it *they cease to be so*." It is fashionable to "talk of the spread of education" and to assert equal treatment for all. Yet fashionable talk will not change the hard fact that society is divided into distinct social classes. "Many will say, 'We are just as good as they are, and as respectable.' So YOU ARE, but yet not fit companions for each other."

Writing around the same time as Day, Fanny Trollope contended that it is simply impossible for civility to exist without traditional markers of good breeding and status. As she argued in her best-selling *Domestic Manners of the Americans*, belief in equality encourages a "coarse familiarity, untempered by any shadow of respect, which is assumed by the grossest and the lowest in their intercourse with the highest and most refined." Trollope tartly concluded, "the theory of equality may be very daintily discussed by English gentlemen in a London dining-room, when the servant, having placed a fresh bottle of cool wine on the table, shuts the door, and leaves them to their walnuts and their wisdom; but it will be found less palatable when it presents itself in the shape of a hard greasy paw, and is claimed in accents that breathe less of freedom than of onions and whiskey."

REPRESSIVE CIVILITY

If we reject the hierarchical view of appropriate behavior advanced by Day and Trollope, then we should not lament the repeated failure to achieve a common code of civil conduct. We should instead say the real problem is that the powerful frequently wish to use their preferred version of civility to subdue and control everyone else.

Mill recognized that civility could be employed to silence expression and he denounced the enforcement of polite conventions that "stigmatize those who hold the contrary opinion as bad and immoral men." As we saw earlier, the Anti-Federalists, nineteenth-century female abolitionists and suffragettes, and twentieth-century civil rights activists were all castigated for violating codes of behavior that favored specific elites. In each of these instances accusations of blatant rudeness and outright barbarism were deployed to intimidate those contesting the status quo.

Additional examples of manners-based intimidation are not hard to find. In the 1980s activists attempting to bring attention to the AIDS crisis found their efforts stymied by a standard of decorum that not only looked down on displays of grief and anger in official proceedings, but also discouraged the public discussion of nonheterosexual practices. Members of the direct-action group ACT UP argued that the conventional understanding of respectful conduct hid the emotional ravages of AIDS from public view and at the same time effectively cast shame on sexual minorities. As a result many of those campaigning for a robust government response to AIDS felt they were forced to choose between advancing their cause or behaving appropriately.

Hip-hop and rap artists in the 1980s and 1990s found themselves in an analogous bind when critics vilified their music as vulgar, violent, and unacceptable in polite society. These "civilitarian" critics, as Randall Kennedy called those who excoriated the music in the name of civility, "have fits over 'coarse language,' but homeless families and involuntary unemployment only get a shrug. They focus more indignation on the raunchy lyrics of gangsta rap than the horrific indifference that makes possible the miserable conditions that those lyrics often vividly portray." Rap musicians were told they could achieve respectability only by abandoning their "distinctive argot, clothing, gestures, and worldviews."

A similar dynamic is evident today in the criticism of "tone policing." Feminists who angrily object to sexism, Black Lives Matter protesters who raise loud voices against institutionalized racism, antiwar demonstrators who passionately inveigh against military engagement— all report instances of being told that they should calm down and try being more polite. The demand to moderate demeanor is experienced as a means of deflecting attention from injustice and relocating the problem in the style of complaint. Like the AIDS crusaders and hip-hop musicians of a generation ago, a broad constellation of activists and dissenters now feel they cannot express themselves without being called uncivil.

Talk of civility's repressive use has even made the national news. In the summer of 2014 Steven Salaita was transitioning from his tenured faculty position at Virginia Tech to a new faculty position, also tenured, at the University of Illinois at Urbana–Champaign. During that same summer, fighting raged between Israeli troops and Palestinians in Gaza. Salaita was upset by the conflict and he aired his views on Twitter, a number of his tweets strongly condemning the Israeli government and Zionism

("At this point, if Netanyahu appeared on TV with a necklace made from the teeth of Palestinian children, would anybody be surprised?"; "Zionists: transforming 'antisemitism' from something horrible into something honorable since 1948").

University of Illinois officials learned of Salaita's tweets and moved to rescind his job offer. As Chancellor Phyllis Wise explained, the decision was made wholly in response to the incivility of Salaita's language: "What we cannot and will not tolerate at the University of Illinois are personal and disrespectful words or actions that demean and abuse either viewpoints themselves or those who express them." The university's president and the board of trustees staunchly supported the chancellor's defense of good manners and pledged to work "to ensure that our university is recognized for its commitment to academic freedom and as a national model of leading-edge scholarship framed in respect and courtesy."

Salaita's firing ignited an intense public controversy. Sixteen of the university's academic departments cast votes of no confidence in the administration and over five thousand scholars signed on to a University of Illinois boycott. The university's Committee on Academic Freedom and Tenure urged the chancellor to disavow the notion that "the incivility of a candidate's utterance may constitute sufficient grounds" for revoking a faculty appointment. And in its public censure of the university the American Association of University Professors (AAUP) argued that "it is always the powerful who determine" incivility's meaning—"a meaning that serves to delegitimize the words and actions of those to whom it is applied." Salaita was simply another nonconformist to be considered unacceptably rude for challenging conventional beliefs.

CIVILITY AS A MEANS OF COMMUNICATION

If civility is opposed to free speech—and if civility is at best superfluous in a vibrant democratic society, and at worst a strong-arm tactic used by repressive elites—then who needs it?

To begin answering this question, we should note that in many instances those who decry civility's coercive use are not opposed to the general idea of civil conduct. Although Mill severely criticized the wielding of civility against those holding minority views, he also welcomed rules of temperate speech and fair discussion that applied equally to all, "giving merited honor to everyone, whatever opinion he may hold." Beginning in 2014, Black Lives Matter activists and their sympathetic allies convulsed college campuses around the country with obstreperous demonstrations, but their ultimate goal was not to destroy civility. The protestors' most common demands, as tallied by FiveThirtyEight.com, were to increase the diversity of faculty and to extend existing campus programs to include diversity training. These are demands for inclusion and recognition. The protestors did not altogether dispense with codes of appropriate behavior so much as they sought to revise prevailing practices in order to foster equal treatment and a sense of belonging for people of color.

In a similar vein, even as it declared civility to be a tool of the powerful, the AAUP report defending Salaita was written in a civil tone. The report also commended the University of Illinois faculty and administration for treating the AAUP subcommittee with courtesy. The AAUP's commitment to civility reaches well beyond any single report. In its foundational "1940 Statement of Principles on Academic Freedom and Tenure," the AAUP suggested that university faculty had something of a "special obligation" to be civil when speaking or writing as ordinary citizens. Because of their position as "members of a learned profession" and as "officers of an educational institution," faculty "should remember that the public may judge their profession and their institution by their utterances" and thus "they should at all times be accurate, should exercise appropriate restraint, [and] should show respect for the opinions of others." Taking AAUP's history into account, we can say that the organization objects to the uses of civility that marginalize and exclude outspoken faculty, but does not deny the value of civility itself.

But why should the AAUP or Mill or any other dissenter be interested in a more inclusive and egalitarian form of civility? Why not simply advocate unrestrained expression?

It turns out that civility offers something that proponents of free speech themselves desire. As Aristotle observed centuries ago, persuasive rhetoric entails sound logical reasoning, targeted emotional appeals, and effective representation of the speaker's integrity and credibility. Yet in a society committed to free expression, people

are at liberty to ignore the elements of persuasiveness that
Aristotle identified. It is perfectly permissible for speakers
to spout illogical arguments, to anger the very audiences
they wish to please, and to present a poor image of their
own character. Failed rhetorical sallies are, as we have
seen, the means by which the free trade in ideas moves
toward truth—but that does not mean such failures are
easy to endure when they are one's own. It is particularly
painful when we project character defects through our
free expression. After all, each of us wants to think of
ourselves as being a good person and we all want others
to regard us in the same way. The chance to come across
as disreputable and morally deficient is not a chance people are generally eager to take. (Or at least the great
majority of us are reluctant to take this chance—as the
philosopher Aaron James details in *Assholes: A Theory*,
there is a type of person who cares very little about what
others think.) The problem with free speech is that it
constantly exposes us to the risk of being seen in a negative light. It is here that civility can be of service.

As Erasmus argued in his enormously popular six-
teenth-century handbook *De Civilitate Morum Puerilium*
(On good manners for children), civility is an essential
form of "outward honesty" that makes inner virtues publicly visible. Civil conduct is a simple, easily employed
means of conveying integrity and moral standing, a way
of behaving that guarantees we are portraying ourselves
positively. With appropriate words and actions, the civil
person grants basic respect and consideration to others. At
the same time, the use of appropriate words and actions

also signals that the civil person is worthy of receiving basic respect and consideration herself. In short, good manners communicate our goodness. "I do not deny that decorum is a very crude part of philosophy," Erasmus wrote, "but in the present climate of opinion it is very conducive to winning good will and to commending those illustrious gifts of the intellect to the eyes of men."

This understanding of civility's communicative value has been picked up by modern authorities. The eminent sociologist Erving Goffman argued that signals sent by good manners identify individuals with whom one may productively interact. Although the restrictions and behavioral modifications dictated by etiquette may seem trivial, civility's requirements broadcast important messages and provide the source materials from which, as Goffman put it, "the gossamer reality of social occasions is built." Along similar lines, Peggy Post, Emily Post's great-granddaughter-in-law and a director of the Emily Post Institute, has written that civility and courtesy are "in essence, the outward expressions of human decency." And the philosopher Cheshire Calhoun has developed the same idea at length, explaining how conformance to civility provides a formula for displaying soundness of character.

We can see the communicative power of civility at work whenever people gather to eat. One might think that table manners are a relatively unimportant matter, at most concerned with good hygiene. Yet the sharing of food with others is an important public act and the style in which we dine transmits important messages about the sort of people we are. During the Middle Ages, as Norbert Elias argued, it was considered appropriate for people to freely express their passions in public, subject only to a few blunt controls. Table manners of the time provided a means for displaying that one was acceptably (that is, loosely) constrained: "Eating from the same plate or dish as others [was] taken for granted. One must only refrain from falling on the dish like a pig, and from dipping bitten food into the communal sauce." As the idea of more finely calibrated and controlled public behavior gained currency, the gradual development of rules for using spoons, forks, individual plates, and napkins offered new ways of projecting one's more delicate and refined qualities. Dining etiquette has never been merely a matter of cleanliness; instead, it has always been a language for communicating information about our trustworthy disposition and our social belonging. "Someone whose table manners differ from our own is someone we may find a little unnerving," Henry Hitchings writes. "'If he eats a tomato like that, what else is he capable of . . . ?'"

We can also see civility's communicative capacity at work in the United States Congress, home to one of the oldest forms of civility in American public life. As the communications scholar Kathleen Hall Jamieson has documented, Congress is institutionally committed to a code of appropriate conduct, the roots of which can be traced back to the procedural rules of order adopted by the House of Representatives in 1789. These rules of order require members of Congress to concentrate on the topic of the debate, not on the personalities of the participants.

The "speakers do not address each other but rather the chair ('Mr. Speaker')" and "they speak of each other as representatives of a state ('the gentlelady from . . . ') not as spokespersons for a party or a position." The governing presumptions behind the rules are that every view is "legitimate even if not correct, and [that] those on all sides are persons of good will and integrity motivated by conviction." Whatever opinion they may happen to voice, members of Congress who maintain decorum can be assured that they are presenting themselves as individuals who warrant appropriate treatment in the legislative chamber.

It is just this sort of assurance that is sought by many who decry the oppressive limitations of conventional civility. Mill envisioned a "real morality of public discussion" that would embrace and recognize every speaker, including the most marginalized nonconformist. Black Lives Matter activists in their most common demands called for reforms that would promote equal standing for people of color in the campus community. The AAUP insisted that Salaita be considered as a worthy participant in university life, without Salaita being forced to alter his opinions about the Middle East. All want what congressional representatives and elegant dining companions have long had: a shared means of interaction that allows participants to show that they are good and decent people, even as they may argue and disagree.

Viewed from this angle, the relationship between free speech and civility takes on a new dimension. Codes of conduct can certainly function as barriers to free expression and as safeguards of status-quo power relations. At the same time, civility also underwrites the effective exchange of ideas by giving individuals a ready means of projecting integrity and good character. We can catalog the instances in which liberty of thought and action collide with norms of appropriate behavior. Yet we must also recognize that many loud complaints about particular rules of decorum are ultimately attempts to refashion etiquette so that it may be put to new use. Free expression battles against civility, and free expression creates a need for civility. Both halves of this contradictory dynamic are always at work, rules of appropriate behavior being openly denounced and busily reconstructed all at the same time.

THE INEVITABILITY OF EGALITARIAN MANNERS?

"Everyone makes manners, building or breaking them at will," Mark Caldwell writes in *A Short History of Rudeness.* "With equal participation from everyone, manners never stabilize, but cycle incessantly worsening or disintegrating in one context, re-forming themselves in another." Civility, like all forms of manners today, is made by many hands, without the control of official institutions or authorized leaders. As society grows more heterogeneous and complex, conceptions of civility shift, come into conflict, and resolve into new forms.

We have seen that the movement is often toward more inclusive and egalitarian standards of decency as civility is recast in terms that permit a broader population to signal their equal worth and standing. Yet it is also important to emphasize that the movement may be in the opposite direction too, with groups advocating new pecking-order rules that assign others to a subordinate rank. As manners rise, fall, and reform, they do not inevitably progress in the direction of egalitarianism.

In hierarchical civility the channels through which individuals communicate their good character feed into a social order where each class has its particular place. Under the racial etiquette of Jim Crow segregation, for instance, African Americans were subject to restrictive codes of appropriate behavior that, when complied with, ensured the privileged status of whites. Today we see a similar dynamic at work in various efforts to displace "political correctness" with new conceptions of manners that vault new groups into a preferred social position.

We have already encountered one contemporary example of tiered manners in the Trump campaign's repeated attempts to downgrade the allegedly inflated level of respect that has previously been shown to Mexican immigrants, Muslims, and women. Another such example is the "Gamergate" controversy, an orchestrated campaign of online harassment that began in 2014 and was directed against female video game developers and feminist critics of sexist video game tropes. The aim of the Gamergate campaign, which included months of anonymous death and rape threats, was to attack the supposedly preferential treatment that was being given to women as gameplay expanded beyond its predominately male base. In a crude and aggressive fashion, Gamergate supporters sought to reset the boundaries of acceptable behavior within the gaming community, forcefully insisting that the only respectable role for women in video gaming was to support male dominance and control.

Gamergate resonates with a broader men's rights movement that traces its contemporary origins to the writings of Warren Farrell. According to Farrell, the preeminence of men in American society masks a reality of male exploitation. Men generally earn more money than women, for example, but this is only because men are expected to be the primary breadwinners in their families and they therefore feel compelled to pursue the most stressful, highest-paying work. Men are left with the empty markers of success, while women possess the true power of self-determination and the capacity to decide how they will be served. "Women are the only minority group that is a majority, the only group that calls themselves oppressed who can control who gets into every office in every community in the country," Farrell argues. "Power is not in who holds the office. Power is in who chooses who holds the office." The basic standards of appropriate behavior must be upended to curtail the inordinate power of women and to free men from the social obligations that prevent them from taking control of their own lives. The hidden truth, Farrell contends, is that men have been effectively enslaved. "When slaves give up their seats for Whites, we call that subservient; when men give up their seats for women we call it politeness."

At the level of general principle many Americans support the idea of equality; as Miss Manners notes, she constantly receives letters from people who declare that they are "just as good as anyone else." In actual practice, however, there is no guarantee that civil behavior will be organized on equal terms. Rules of civility always provide a means of communicating good character, but the rules need not assign everyone an equal station. And whatever measure of equality may be achieved in polite society at one point is no assurance that some people will not try to reassert hierarchy at a later date. The nineteenth-century revision of female respectability allowed independent women to advocate their political interests without causing scandal, but this did not prevent movements to subordinate women from emerging in our own time.

To achieve and sustain egalitarian civility, we must advocate it through our speech and model it in our actions. Like any advocacy in a free society, the push for egalitarian civility will generate pushback. Disagreement can be expected from those who insist that real equality is a matter of removing the "special privileges" purportedly enjoyed by historically disenfranchised groups like racial minorities, dissenting religions, recent immigrants, and women. Disagreement can also be expected from those who adhere to older standards of civility through habit, and from those who simply choose to follow their own idiosyncratic understandings of good manners. Even among people who endorse the same vision of egalitarian civility, we should expect disputes over questions of application.

Establishing a more inclusionary code of conduct requires persistent effort, and in our diverse and dynamic society there is no hope that anything like complete compliance will ever be achieved. The effort is nonetheless worthwhile in order to prevent inegalitarian alternatives from gaining ground. If we recall that civility forms the baseline of decent behavior, and that its rules set out the terms of social belonging and identify the basic forms of consideration we owe one another in public life, then we will see that the work of improving civility is of great importance, even if this work is difficult and never completely finished.

Civility presents us with vast opportunity. As we attempt to forge standards of appropriate behavior, we can influence the negotiation of the thousands of public interactions that make up ordinary life. With this great opportunity comes great responsibility to ensure that the etiquette we seek to establish is fit for a free and equal people.

Civility gives us a highly valuable method for publicizing our good character. Yet this great virtue is accompanied by a glaring vice: the messages that civility communicates can easily be faked.

The possibility of inauthenticity was spotted early. In the sixteenth century, when Erasmus began trumpeting the value of civility as a kind of "outward honesty" that made inner goodness publicly visible, critics complained that individuals might manipulate codes of appropriate behavior for their own advantage. As Anna Bryson explains in her study of early modern civility, "once manners are conceived of as representational, they can also be regarded as theatrical and even dissimulatory." There was little to prevent "the vicious or talentless man" from using "representational techniques to project absent merits."

John Kasson finds the same concern with false display in the nineteenth-century United States. The idea that good manners could convey true character was a powerful inducement for Americans of the time to learn how to behave, not only because polite learning would permit an individual to advertise her own virtues but also because knowledge of civility's requirements would allow residents of the teeming urban centers to discern a "solid gentleman." The difficulty was that very different sorts of people could exhibit good manners. As a result nineteenth-century Americans found it tough to tell when the information broadcast by civil behavior was genuine and when it was a sham, and hard to know whether a given individual was in fact a "solid gentleman" of fine quality or a mere "social counterfeit" out for himself. As Kasson notes, it is no coincidence that the term "confidence man" was coined during this period to designate a swindler of "genteel appearance." The fundamental crime of the con man, Erving Goffman once observed, is that he robs the public of the belief that only good people have good manners.

Evidence of ersatz civility abounds today. Consider the artificiality and double dealing of congressional decorum. Members of Congress have adhered to their own code of civil behavior for centuries. When partisans within Congress engage in heated debate, however, the decorous expressions of admiration required by the chamber's rules barely conceal how representatives really feel about one another. A representative may scrupulously follow the proper form of address, praising a learned colleague and honoring the great and bountiful state from which he hails. At the same time, the representative can make clear that she thinks her colleague is a liar and a crook. The rules of order that members of Congress use to communicate genuine mutual respect are the identical rules they use to communicate the mere pretense of mutual respect. And in the actual practice of congressional deliberation today, it often seems as if phony esteem is far more plentiful than the real thing.

It may not be surprising to learn that the words politicians use may ring hollow. But in this instance elected officials faithfully represent ordinary people. The everyday practice of civility, just like the formal practice of more elaborate decorum in the halls of Congress, often appears false. Virtually every rule of civil etiquette involves showing respect for others in some way—with the emphasis placed on "showing." As Miss Manners writes, the respect called for by good manners is a matter of "outward form," an exhibition of "consideration toward everyone and a showing of special deference to those who are older or in a position of authority." Although one might have "genuine admiration" for "someone who has proved himself to be worthy of it," all one need do to be civil is go through the conventional motions of showing respect. Real feeling and deep conviction are certainly compatible with codes of conduct, but they are not essential. Good manners may reflect true personal decency or they merely may reflect the desire to appear truly decent; the genuinely gracious soul and the unrepentant rogue may both be unfailingly polite.

THE MORALITY OF CIVILITY

The charge of hypocrisy is a serious one, perhaps because accusations of hypocrisy have historically been associated with the feigning of religious belief. As grave as the charge may be, hypocrisy nonetheless does seem to be what is taking place in polite society. Insincerity, for example, refers to a general type of dishonesty or lack of genuineness, the assuming of any false guise in speech or action. Hypocrisy, by contrast, denotes a more specific kind of pretense: the hypocrite is someone who pretends to have feelings or beliefs superior to his real ones. An insincere person can simulate kindness or cruelty, but the hypocrite by definition is more constrained. To be a hypocrite one must pretend to be better than one actually is. And that is precisely what happens when people use civility to publicize positive qualities of character they do not possess. What is to be done?

One response is to insist that civility is a species of morality. The treatment of civility as a moral virtue does not of course prevent individuals from hypocritically deploying manners for their own selfish purposes. But it does allow those asserting civility's moral status to claim that hypocritical manners are not really good manners at all. "If politeness is a quality of character (alongside courtesy, good manners and civility), it cannot be a flaw," P. M. Forni writes. "A suave manipulator may appear to be polite but is not." In a similar vein Edward Shils argues in *The Virtue of Civility* that genuine "substantive civility" self-consciously places the interests of the whole society above the interests of the part. "Civility is a virtue expressed in action on behalf of the whole society, on behalf of the good of all members of the society to which public liberties and representative institutions are integral." To be truly civil, just as to be truly honest or truly good, requires the intentional enactment of specific values. Those who deploy manners as a false front are simply failing to be civil.

The moral approach to civility is understandable, not only as an attempt to purge hypocrisy from the realm of manners but also as an indication that people do indeed relate to civility in normative terms. When we talk about how to demonstrate our own goodness, or when we discuss how to treat others as ends rather than as mere means, we often point to our understanding of what constitutes civil behavior. Codes of appropriate conduct clearly operate in a moral register. Even so, it is a mistake to treat manners and morality as identical.

Civility remains fundamentally an activity of outward display. Personal intentions matter a great deal in morality, and they hardly matter at all in manners. A person performing a moral action for the wrong reasons is considered to be immoral. By contrast a person acting civilly is considered to be civil regardless of her motives. Civility is as civility does. To insist to the contrary that civility requires purity of intention is to ignore the fact that in actual practice civility is treated as a matter of following appropriate forms. As Erving Goffman noted, it is the person who conforms to the conventions of good manners—by striving "to fit in and act as persons of his kind are expected to act"—who reveals the "least amount of information about himself" in any social gathering. Civility permits public action while screening private beliefs, allowing everyone to be well mannered regardless of their underlying desires or character. The opportunity for concealment is not an incidental feature of civility; instead it is an essential part of the experience of being in civilized company.

Lord Chesterfield, the great eighteenth-century champion of civility and polished manners, saw frequent need to obscure true feelings: "In the course of the world, a man must very often put on an easy, frank countenance, upon very disagreeable occasions; he must seem pleased when he is very much otherwise; he must be able to accost and receive with smiles those whom he would much rather meet with swords." The well-bred gentleman, "like the Chameleon," must "be able to take every different hue."

As an example of moral reasoning Chesterfield's observations may be unacceptable—Dr. Johnson, for instance, thought that Chesterfield's writings showcased "the morals of a whore." But Chesterfield was not writing a moral treatise. He was instead describing how good manners actually functioned. In this endeavor Chesterfield proved to be highly successful. Since their debut in 1774, his letters on the "Art of Becoming a Man of the World and a Gentleman" have been repeatedly republished (including as an e-book in 2015) and continue to be read.

Modern manners mavens often echo Chesterfield. They acknowledge that civility distances external behavior from internal beliefs and, in doing so, leaves open the possibility that civil individuals do not really mean what they say. As her biographer notes, Emily Post consistently gave the same simple advice whenever facing a choice between telling the "bare truth" and behaving appropriately: everyone should always choose to be courteous and polite. Miss Manners frames the same idea in different terms: because manners are meant to be used by everyone, it will be the case that "really mean people get the advantage of practicing ingratiating behavior."

There is a second line of argument that might be used to claim good manners are effectively moral. Civility involves a degree of habituation—a fact that is illustrated by etiquette manuals directed at parents and the subject of child-rearing. The cultivation of habits in children is chiefly a matter of parental guidance and repetition. Elders must first model civil conduct, giving the young a pattern of behavior to observe and imitate. Once exemplary behavior has been enacted, parents must then repeatedly exhort and admonish children to perform like adults.

Many have suggested that the continuous drill of courtesy lessons enforced by parental say-so might eventually lead to something like the sincere embrace of substantive virtues. The idea that repeated action might produce some elements of genuine conviction has been endorsed in varying degrees by figures ranging from Thomas Jefferson ("In truth, politeness is artificial good humor, it covers the natural want of it, and ends by rendering habitual a substitute nearly equivalent to the real virtue") to Miss Manners ("If you write enough thank-you letters, you may actually come to feel a flicker of gratitude"). Benjamin Franklin advocated this idea of virtue-via-habit throughout his life. Franklin saw the self as "a constellation of passions and interests," a disorderly composite of impulses and appetites which made it unlikely that individuals would act on the basis of pure and virtuous motives. Given these circumstances, the best bet was to shape the self "into a productive whole through good habits." Thus Franklin was, as his biographer notes, committed to a simple proposition: "*do* the right thing, and in time you will learn to *want* to do the right thing."

Yet even though one might say that authentic goodness is the ultimate goal of good habits, it remains the case that good manners do not depend on individuals actually becoming more or less who they are pretending to be. Childhood is a propitious time to inculcate appropriate behavior precisely because the young need not be persuaded about the inherent rightness of any particular values; the goal is simply to make them act civilly. As Erasmus wrote, "Young bodies resemble young shoots, which come to maturity and require the fixed characteristics of whatever you determine for them with a pole or trellis." Or as Miss Manners put the point more recently, etiquette is "best taught at the start of life, when learning without conviction is easiest."

The habits of civility are, at base, habits of action. Childhood training produces adults disposed to follow the conventions of etiquette and who can be shamed whenever they stray from the path of politeness. Such adults are committed to particular routines of conduct and need not actually accept the substantive ideas of concern and respect that the routines may be considered to express. Habit conditions individuals to adhere to form, preparing them for a practice of civility that is (as we have already seen) largely a matter of external display rather than a reflection of inner intentions. Broad habituation to the same standards of behavior does yield important community benefits. And at the individual level habit may ultimately generate morally correct motives. Yet habit need not instill good motives in everyone for good manners to prevail. Nor will habit prevent hypocritical manipulation from occurring should an individual decide to use civility to create misleadingly favorable appearances.

THE POSITIVE VALUE OF HYPOCRISY

Civility provides a way of expressing our own good character and due consideration for others; at the same time, civility is also always open to hypocritical use. Many see value in the communicative power of civility, but this positive evaluation rarely extends to the possibility of hypocrisy. Hypocrisy is, as we know, a plainly pejorative term. We are very reluctant to find hypocrisy in our own behavior. "I am no more likely to identify myself as a hypocrite," Jenny Davidson notes in her study of hypocrisy and politeness, "than I am to call myself a cannibal." And when we detect hypocrisy in others we are often quick to criticize, even when the duplicity in question is neither particularly egregious nor malicious. As David Runciman finds in his historical analysis of hypocrisy, the slightest perception of pretense can provoke strong reactions when the pretending is done by people we do not like.

Hypocrisy is negative, to be sure, and the discovery that people are engaged in pretense can be toxic. This helps explain the appeal of figures like Donald Trump who promise straight talk. In place of the artificial conventions found in any code of appropriate conduct, truth tellers of various stripes boldly voice opinions that have been silenced and refuse to kowtow to rules that mask real feelings. In a society filled with poseurs, it is refreshing to come across individuals who are not afraid to tell it like it is.

However, the goal of many critics of good manners is not to break free from civility altogether but to establish new forms of civility that offer new ways of communicating standing and belonging. These new civilities have their own artificial conventions that are inevitably open to hypocritical manipulation and subject to the criticism of inauthenticity. In the case of Trump, for instance, his success on the campaign trail was attended by suspicion that his brand of blunt talk and his insistence on a new social hierarchy were merely poses struck for the sake of personal advancement. Such suspicions were fueled by the belief that Trump might ultimately abandon his controversial campaign style in order to appear more conventionally presidential. It did not help that Trump's campaign chief, Paul Manafort, defended the possibility of a new political persona in terms that would have pleased Chesterfield. "You can't change somebody's character," Manafort observed. "But you can change the way somebody presents themselves."

All of this suggests that hypocrisy is a permanent liability and always a potential source of civility's undoing.

But are all the properties of hypocritical behavior necessarily negative? Are there conditions in which hypocrisy's poison also works as a cure?

Judith Shklar believed that such conditions exist right here in the United States. Shklar argued that American society is an irreducibly diverse and unruly assemblage of passionate, conflict-prone individuals: "We do not agree on the facts and figures of social life, and we heartily dislike one another's religious, sexual, intellectual, and political commitments—not to mention one another's ethnic, racial and class character." Social peace and mutual accommodation are nonetheless possible in such a context, not because the populace will actually be moved by a common set of moral convictions but because there are opportunities for acting in ways that disguise our true beliefs and interests. "The democracy of everyday life, which is rightly admired by egalitarian visitors to America, does not arise from sincerity," Shklar wrote. "It is based on the pretense that we must speak to each other as if social standings were a matter of indifference in our views of each other. That is, of course, not true. Not all of us are even convinced that all men are entitled to a certain minimum of social respect."

The reliance on pretense does not sit easily with the importance assigned to public moral standards, and many people may prefer not to dwell on the contrived posturing that facilitates social interaction. Even so, the reliance on pretense remains whether or not individuals are comfortable acknowledging it. Rather than being a corruption of true civility, hypocrisy is a means by which good manners become useful in a society in which almost no one can live up to collective ideals.

Shklar is not alone in thinking that civility thrives because of hypocritical posturing rather than merely in spite of it. In her book *Hypocrisy and Integrity*, Ruth Grant develops an argument that generalizes Shklar's assessment of everyday democracy in America. Grant notes that within an ideal world of true intimates, where everyone who depends on one another has perfectly aligned interests, hypocrisy is utterly destructive. In the actual world of community life, however, where the people who depend on one another often have conflicting interests, hypocritical behavior helps "false friends" make useful arrangements without requiring deep agreement or genuine affinity.

People in a civil society, Grant writes, "are not treated according to their individual merits or their just desserts, nor according to one's true feelings toward them as individuals, but according to conventional forms." These conventional courtesies "allow civic public relations between people who are not friends," offering practical ways for people to interact without requiring the terms of each meeting to be negotiated from scratch or obliging individuals to be connected by true affection. Civility endures because it does not require personal goals to coincide or good feelings to prevail. Regardless of what individuals actually think about one another, civility holds out the promise that people will live in harmony simply if they are well mannered. The suspicion that polite tokens of respect are fake (either in Congress or in ordinary life) may be an indication that someone is trying to exploit good manners for their own selfish advantage. Yet the same suspicion is also an indication of civility successfully operating—a matter of individuals going along for the sake of getting along.

The idea that hypocrisy helps make civility useful depends on a specific understanding of the human condition. First of all, to accept that polite pretense provides a way of ensuring social coordination, one must believe that the differences in individual beliefs and interests are significant and irreducible. If everyone could somehow be trained or persuaded to adopt the same views and advance the same interests, then there would be no need to seek any techniques for managing diversity and disagreement.

Beyond accepting heterogeneity and conflict as unalterable facts, one must also believe that ordinary people are governed by an inextricable mix of high principle and low passion. Moral standards are an essential part of social life. Such standards form the basis of communal ties, provide a means for restraining destructive impulses, and furnish a set of ideals to which community members aspire. "Public discourse is conducted in moral terms, and that shared language is itself part of the constitution of any particular public," Grant writes. Thus one must consider it to be impossible for people to permanently set aside moral principle for the sake of interactions anchored solely in self-interest. As individuals go about their business, they not only "want to be thought of as good" but also "want to think of themselves as good."

We have seen that this desire to project moral integrity attracts people to civility as a means of communication. The case for hypocrisy's constructive role requires us to add a complication: although people aspire to moral ideals, public life cannot ultimately be run on the basis of morality. People are often motivated by ambition, pride, and vanity; as a result they will never be completely able to practice the high principles that they preach. Public moral standards remain important, as does the inclination to follow them. Individuals are, however, typically too consumed with self-love to actually uphold these moral standards and will seek shortcuts whenever they can. As Grant puts it, "because society requires morality but men are not always moral, hypocrisy is inevitable." Rather than actually being good, individuals will strive for the appearance of goodness in the hope of making a positive impression. People value collective ideals even though they cannot always live up to them, and systems of moral principle remain important ordering mechanisms even if no one can consistently conform to their terms.

Grant traces this mixed portrait of human proclivities to Machiavelli. We can find elements of the same understanding in the maxims of La Rochefoucauld, who wrote that "hypocrisy is a tribute that vice pays to virtue" and "social life would not last long if men were not taken in by each other." A similar thread of reasoning is present in the writings of Edmund Burke, who praised "pleasing illusions" of sentiment and tradition that cover "the defects of our naked, shivering nature" so that "the fierceness of pride and power" may be subdued and "the different shades of life" may be harmonized.

The same thinking is also deep within American history. James Madison believed that individuals were capable of some goodness, that there were "qualities in human nature which justify a certain portion of esteem and confidence." But Madison also believed that there is a "degree of depravity in mankind which requires a certain degree of circumspection and distrust." Because man's "reason and self-love" are bound up together, "his opinions and his passions will have a reciprocal influence on each other." The result is a "zeal for different opinions" that has "divided mankind into parties, inflamed them with mutual animosity, and rendered them much more disposed to vex and oppress each other than to co-operate for their common good." Thus Madison argued that any plan to establish a new political order must take people for the intensely passionate, highly self-interested, and only occasionally virtuous creatures that they are.

Following this line of thinking from Machiavelli to Madison, we arrive at the conclusion that ordinary people are at once ethically attuned, willful, and vain. Civility becomes valuable because it allows us to trade on significant yet often unobtainable moral standards, permitting us to call for expressions of concern and mutual respect without necessarily requiring very much in the way of actual virtue. Civility does not attempt to untangle the threads of principle and passion that run through each person. Instead civility provides a code of behavior and a set of conventions that channel human contradictions in

socially productive directions, making possible coopera-
tion and mutual benefit where one would otherwise
expect empty moral gestures, self-seeking actions, and
conflict. As David Runciman writes, hypocritical practices like civility offer a kind of "coping mechanism for
the problem of vice," furnishing forms of concealment
that permit people "to be better than they might be" by
giving them the opportunity to pretend to be better than
they are. Civility is useful precisely because it allows for
hypocritical posturing. Indeed it might even be said, as
Jenny Davidson suggests, that being recognized as a mem-
ber of polite society gives one "the right to be hypocritical" by enabling participation in civility's pretenses.

Advocates of good manners have long argued along
these very lines. Lord Chesterfield admitted that "the
strictest and most scrupulous honor and virtue alone can
make you esteemed by mankind." And yet such moral
rectitude will not make an individual "liked, beloved, and
sought after" in life. Why is this so? Since people value
virtue, one might say that it is reasonable to assume that
good morals should be sufficient for personal success. This
assumption turns out to be unwarranted, Chesterfield
argued, because reason does not firmly govern the passions and appetites embedded in human nature. "Reason
ought to direct the whole, but seldom does. And he who
addresses himself singly to another man's reason, without
endeavoring to engage his heart in his interest also, is no
more likely to succeed, than a man who should apply only
to a King's nominal minister, and neglect his favorite."
Civility, politeness, and courtesy are therefore "absolutely

necessary to adorn any, or all other good qualities or talents." Good manners create a pleasant facade that allows life to proceed without irritation or conflict—a fact made plain by the interactions among European aristocrats. Royal courts "are, unquestionably, the seats of politeness and good-breeding," Chesterfield wrote, and "were they not so, they would be the seats of slaughter and desolation. Those who now smile upon and embrace, would affront and stab each other, if manners did not interpose; but ambition and avarice, the two prevailing passions at courts, found dissimulation more effectual than violence; and dissimulation introduced the habit of politeness."

In our own day Miss Manners has similarly claimed that good manners obscure and soften the strife produced whenever individuals try to live side by side. Miss Manners frequently reminds her readers that people do not naturally get along. To argue that they will get along if they just get to know one another "trivializes intellectual, emotional, and spiritual convictions by characterizing any difference between one person's and another's as no more than a simple misunderstanding, easily resolved by frank exchanges or orchestrated 'encounters.'" It is the hypocrisy of civility—the insistence that individuals conform to an artificial code of decent behavior whether or not they actually like one another—that is necessary to make social peace and smooth interaction possible, without unrealistically attempting to reconcile stubborn conflicts or romantically wishing away deep disagreements. Honest communication has far less promise of producing social coordination, even though "hardly anyone would dispute the proposition that morals are more important than manners." Were the virtue of truth telling to be widely and consistently practiced, everyone would have license to hurt one another's feelings and we would end up with people shouting at each other in the streets. "It turns out," Miss Manners concludes, "that dear old hypocrisy, inhibitions and artificiality, daintily wrapped in a package called etiquette, were protecting us from forms of natural behavior that even the most vehement opponents of etiquette find intolerable."

PITTING PASSION AGAINST PASSION

There is a very old school of thought that claims human reason is insufficient to cabin and control human passions. Reason can be used to justify plans for social coordination and mutually useful accommodation, the thinking goes, but rational justification will not succeed on its own because reason does not firmly govern our impulses and appetites. "Rationality is a bond between persons," the philosopher Stuart Hampshire has observed, "but it is not a very powerful bond and it is apt to fail as a bond when there are strong passions on two sides of a conflict." This failure of reason is bound to occur on a regular basis because we live in communities with great diversity and intense disagreement. Our different needs, histories, ambitions, and vanities all conspire to keep us zealously engaged in endless disputes.

The centuries-old argument about the weakness of reason touched off a search for more effective constraints that long ago led to what Albert Hirschman called the "principle of the countervailing passions": to "fight fire with fire" by using "one set of comparatively innocuous passions to countervail another more dangerous or destructive set." The discovery that desires and drives could be used to play a countervailing role was hailed as a great advance, a "message of hope" that there was a way to thread the needle between the "destructiveness of passion and the ineffectuality of reason."

Civility operates in this tradition of thought and steers deleterious passions into appropriate channels by enlisting a measure of habituation along with the powerful desire to appear to be better than one actually is. One can certainly make reasoned arguments in favor of a given code of conduct. But civility, like all schemes of countervailing passions, seeks predictability and peace in an inconstant, conflict-ridden world by not relying on rational justification alone.

An indicator of civility's success in making use of passion is the pleasure that we take from surfaces and display when good manners are in place. Burke had the beautifying effects of refined manners and "ancient chivalry" in mind when he mourned the great losses wrought by the French Revolution: "It is gone, that sensibility of principle, that chastity of honor which felt a stain like a wound, which inspired courage whilst it mitigated ferocity, which ennobled whatever it touched, under which vice itself lost half its evil by losing all of its grossness." Good manners lend a veneer of grace and sophistication to life, stimulating attachments to attractive display. (Arguing in a similar vein, Oscar Wilde would later observe that "what is interesting about people in good society . . . is the mask that each one of them wears, not the reality that lies behind the mask.") Burke could not support the French revolutionaries because they had stripped the public sphere of its tasteful and elegant gilding, and in doing so had eliminated a critical means of engaging citizen affections. "There ought be a system of manners in every nation which a well-informed mind would be disposed to relish," Burke wrote. "To make us love our country, our country ought to be lovely."

Like Burke, Chesterfield also understood the surface pleasures of good manners and he connected these surface pleasures directly to the desire to appear better than one is. A "mistaken self-love" is harmful, Chesterfield wrote, because it induces individuals to "take the immediate and indiscriminate gratification of a passion, or appetite, for real happiness." By contrast a sensible self-love is the defining characteristic of civilized company. "If a man has a mind to be thought wiser, and a woman handsomer, than they really are, their error is a comfortable one to themselves, and an innocent one with regard to other people; and I would rather make them my friends by indulging them in it, than my enemies by endeavoring (and that to no purpose) to undeceive them." Chesterfield argued that it was of no use lamenting the fact that sensible self-love drives people to place so much stock in such shallow talk, for the "world is taken by the outside of things, and we must take the world as it is; you or I cannot set it right." Besides, the way of the world makes the pleasures of good manners available to everyone. The reciprocal practice of civility allows each to appease the vanities of the other, binding hearts to the conventions of good manners. Thus it is not only useful to be civil; it also feels good. "Pleasing in company," Chesterfield noted, "is the only way of being pleased in it yourself."

The same reasoning suffuses Dale Carnegie's classic text on business manners and sales technique, *How to Win Friends and Influence People*. Originally published in 1936, Carnegie's manual on how to properly conduct commercial relations has sold over fifteen million copies and its principles have been propounded in countless seminars and courses. Carnegie's view of the highs and lows of human nature would be easily recognized by any devotee of Madison or Miss Manners. "When dealing with people, let us remember we are not dealing with creatures of logic," Carnegie wrote. "We are dealing with creatures of emotion, creatures bristling with prejudices and motivated by pride and vanity." At the same time, Carnegie noted that no one wants to present themselves as being driven by passion and conceit. A "person usually has two reasons for doing a thing: one that sounds good and a real one. The person himself will think of the real reason. You don't need to emphasize that. But all of us, being idealists at heart, like to think of motives that sound good."

How to Win Friends and Influence People provides step-by-step guidance on how to help others feel good about themselves by reflecting back to them their own interests and idealistic understanding of who they are. Business associates will be pleased by the recognition and appreciation they are given. And the individual bestowing the recognition and appreciation will in turn feel gratified for having made others feel valued and important. All parties will then be able to work together for mutual profit and advantage.

Carnegie occasionally worried that this confection of reciprocal pleasing might be seen as mere hypocritical posturing designed to advance one's career. To allay this concern, Carnegie assured his readers that he was not offering "a bag of tricks." "Remember, we all crave appreciation and recognition, and will do almost anything to get it. But nobody wants insincerity. Nobody wants flattery." Carnegie believed that faithful application of his method would eventually transform people from self-involved beings into truly virtuous souls who come to possess the wonderful qualities that have been ascribed to them.

Carnegie's account of bootstrapped virtue is similar to the understanding of habit that some use to frame civility as a form of morality. And as with habit, it might be true that some individuals applying Carnegie's methods will ultimately find their way to authentic moral convictions. Yet we need not wait for moral transformation in order to exploit the rules of appropriate conduct. The pleasures of business manners are available for our enjoyment and use right now. As Carnegie phrased it, "an increased tendency to think always in terms of other people's point of view, and see things from their angle—if you get that one thing out of this book, it may easily prove to be one of the building blocks of your career."

The pleasure of participating in a given form of civility is not of course the only pleasure to be found. A kind of mischievous fun can be had by lampooning or violating established manners. Strategic incivility, as we saw earlier, provokes and manipulates the outrage that results from contravening standards of appropriate behavior. Strategic incivility can also be a source of enjoyment, not only for the offenders who revel in the attention that their rule breaking brings, but also for (at least some) bystanders who get a subversive thrill from seeing proprieties flouted. Trump, our example of a strategic offender, relished his own politically incorrect pronouncements. And Trump's raucous rallies provided ample evidence that certain groups delighted in hearing Trump say what other public figures would not.

Strategic incivility is typically a matter of pursuing short-term advantage, and in most instances the pleasures of complying with prevailing decorum face no risk of being eclipsed by the pleasures of disobedience. Strategic incivility does, however, sometimes play into a push for an altogether new code of conduct (Trump's efforts fall into this camp). In such cases illicit fun becomes bound up with a deeper defiance of convention that ultimately seeks to inaugurate new manners as the preferred means of communicating good character and respect. When a revolution in manners succeeds, those who were once excited by rule violation come to enjoy the stable pleasures of a newly fashioned civility—a civility that, like all the varieties of civility that have been or are yet to come, speaks to the eternal desire to look better than one otherwise may be.

5 STRENGTH IN WEAKNESS

Civility is beset by paradoxes. We feel civility's absence as a result of its abundance. We see civility as an impediment to free expression, and at the same time we demand civility to sustain the free exchange of ideas. We encounter civility as a bulwark of hierarchy and domination, and we also enlist civility to level social relations and promote inclusion. We condemn civility's inauthenticity, yet we depend on the many opportunities for hypocrisy that civility affords.

These contradictions and tensions do not make for a logically consistent system. But then logical consistency is not always a hallmark of enduring social practices.

Consider the ancient rules of monarchical succession favoring eldest sons. Pedigree is no guarantee of talent or skill, and it makes little sense to select individuals for important leadership positions on the basis of lineage. If we are truly committed to rational policy making, surely we should prefer leaders with the best character and experience rather than picking those who happen to have the right parents. And yet, as the seventeenth-century polymath Pascal observed, hereditary monarchy may endure in spite of its seeming absurdity. "For whom will men choose, as the most virtuous and able? We at once come to blows as each claims to be [the best]. Let us then attach this quality to something indisputable. This is the king's eldest son. That is clear and there is no dispute." Given the disputatious tendencies of human nature, the absurdity of selection by kinship is offset by its capacity to secure civil peace. "The most unreasonable things in the world become most reasonable," Pascal concluded, "because of the unruliness of men."

In the very same way, the unsettled state of civility looks reasonable once we account for our own unruliness. We are surrounded by multiple and conflicting claims about the kinds of consideration we owe one another in public life. Rather than witnessing convergence on a fixed and universally accepted etiquette, we see ongoing controversy and ferment, with old codes of appropriate behavior persisting and new codes always arising, and with citizens continually criticizing one another because they find a given set of manners inauthentic or because they believe that a particular mode of civil behavior fails to grant appropriate forms of recognition.

Many commentators consider current conditions to be a crisis and a harbinger of imminent social collapse. By contrast my argument is that the persistent and fractious disagreements over civility reflect the steady cross-pressures of deep structural factors, including the diversity and dynamism of American society, the flourishing of our free speech culture, our desire to be seen as decent and good people, and our frequent inability to live up to the moral principles that give shape and meaning to our lives.

To trace the ongoing battles over civility to underlying causes is not to say that we must simply be resigned to the status quo. The argument made here does require us to dismiss the idea of a golden age, past or future, where a single understanding of civility is firmly established and secure from all challenge. Civility does not exist outside of politics as an independent force that restrains and pacifies our disputes. Instead civility is itself a subject of political struggle and debate, a mode of behavior that is developed and perpetually refashioned in the democracy of everyday life. The need for civility is ever present, and the work of enacting better and more acceptable rules of conduct will always be with us. Recognizing this fact is not a reason to give up so much as it is a call to join in and to embrace the paradoxes on which our efforts to get along depend.

SOURCES AND FURTHER READING

I drew on a variety of materials in my writing and I provide a selected list of sources below. Two works deserve separate mention. First, I should note that I developed some of my ideas about good manners in an earlier book, *All Judges Are Political—Except When They Are Not: Acceptable Hypocrisies and the Rule of Law* (Stanford University Press, 2010). In that book I examined common courtesy as a means of explaining how the American public perceives the courts and the judicial process. Although its primary focus is the rule of law, *All Judges Are Political—Except When They Are Not* informs a number of the arguments in the present work, *How Civility Works*. Second, in addition to consulting the works by Judith Martin (a.k.a. Miss Manners), which I list below, I learned a good deal by reading the *Miss Manners* advice column. Along with her books and articles Martin's thrice-weekly column provides an indispensable map of modern civility's terrain.

Alford, Henry. *Would It Kill You to Stop Doing That? A Modern Guide to Manners*. New York: Twelve, 2012.

American Association of University Professors. "Academic Freedom and Tenure: The University of Illinois at Urbana-Champaign." www.aaup.org/report/UIUC (last accessed June 1, 2016).

———. "1940 Statement of Principles on Academic Freedom and Tenure." www.aaup.org/report/1940 -statement-principles-academic-freedom-and-tenure (last accessed June 1, 2016).

Aristotle. *Rhetoric*, translated by W. Rhys Roberts. http:// classics.mit.edu//Aristotle/rhetoric.html (last accessed June 1, 2016).

Bryson, Anna. *From Courtesy to Civility: Changing Codes of Conduct in Early Modern England*. Oxford: Clarendon Press, 1998.

Burke, Edmund. *Reflections on the Revolution in France*, edited by J.G.A. Pocock. Indianapolis: Hackett, 1987.

Caldwell, Mark. *A Short History of Rudeness*. New York: Picador USA, 1999.

Calhoun, Cheshire. "The Virtue of Civility." *Philosophy and Public Affairs* 29 (2000): 251–76.

Carnegie, Dale. *How to Win Friends and Influence People*. Rev. ed. New York: Pocket Books, 1981, originally published 1936.

Claridge, Laura. *Emily Post: Daughter of the Gilded Age, Mistress of American Manners*. New York: Random House, 2008.

Davidson, Jenny. *Hypocrisy and the Politics of Politeness: Manners and Morals from Locke to Austen.* New York: Cambridge University Press, 2004.

Day, Charles William. *Hints on Etiquette and the Usages of Society with a Glance at Bad Habits,* illustrated by Brian Robb. London: Turnstile Press, 1946, originally published 1834.

Elias, Norbert. "The History of Manners." Vol. 1 of *The Civilizing Process,* translated by Edmund Jephcott. New York: Urizen Books, 1978, originally published 1939.

———. "Power and Civility." Vol. 2 of *The Civilizing Process,* translated by Edmund Jephcott. New York: Pantheon, 1982, originally published 1939.

Erasmus, Desiderius. *De Civilitate Morum Puerilium* (1530), translated by Brian McGregor. In *Literary and Educational Writings 3,* 273–89. Vol. 25 of *Collected Works of Erasmus,* edited by J. K. Sowards. Toronto: University of Toronto Press, 1985.

Farrell, Warren. "The Myth of Male Power: Why Men Are the Disposable Sex, Part I." *New Male Studies* 2 (2012): 4–33.

———. "The Myth of Male Power: Why Men Are the Disposable Sex, Part II." *New Male Studies* 3 (2012): 5–31.

Forni, P. M. *Choosing Civility: The Twenty-Five Rules of Considerate Conduct.* New York: St. Martin's Press, 2002.

Goffman, Erving. *Behavior in Public Places: Notes on the Social Organization of Gatherings.* New York: Free Press, 1963.

———. *The Presentation of Self in Everyday Life*. New York: Anchor, 1959.

Gould, Deborah B. "Life during Wartime: Emotions and the Development of ACT UP." *Mobilization* 7 (2002): 177–200.

Grant, Ruth W. *Hypocrisy and Integrity: Machiavelli, Rousseau, and the Ethics of Politics*. Chicago: University of Chicago Press, 1997.

Hamilton, Alexander, James Madison, and John Jay. *The Federalist Papers*, edited by Clinton Rossiter. New York: Mentor, 1961.

Hampshire, Stuart. *Justice Is Conflict*. Princeton, NJ: Princeton University Press, 2000.

Hart, H.L.A. *The Concept of Law*. 2d ed. New York: Oxford University Press, 1994.

Herbst, Susan. *Rude Democracy: Civility and Incivility in American Politics*. Philadelphia: Temple University Press, 2010.

Hess, Stephen. *The Little Book of Campaign Etiquette: For Everyone with a Stake in Politicians and Journalists*. Washington, DC: Brookings, 1998.

Hirschman, Albert O. *The Passions and the Interests: Political Arguments for Capitalism before Its Triumph*. 20th anniversary ed. Princeton, NJ: Princeton University Press, 1997.

Hitchings, Henry. *Sorry! The English and Their Manners*. New York: Farrar, Straus and Giroux, 2013.

Houston, Alan. *Benjamin Franklin and the Politics of Improvement*. New Haven, CT: Yale University Press, 2008.

James, Aaron. *Assholes: A Theory*. New York: Anchor, 2014.

Jamieson, Kathleen Hall. "Civility in the House of Representatives." March 1, 1997, www.annenbergpublic policycenter.org/civility-in-the-house-of-representatives/ (last accessed June 1, 2016).

Kasson, John F. *Rudeness and Civility: Manners in Nineteenth-Century Urban America*. New York: Hill and Wang, 1990.

Kennedy, Randall. "State of the Debate: The Case against 'Civility.'" *American Prospect*, November–December 1998, www.prospect.org/cs/articles?article=the_case_against_civility (last accessed June 1, 2016).

King, Martin Luther, Jr. "Letter from a Birmingham Jail." April 16, 1963, www.africa.upenn.edu/Articles_Gen/Letter_Birmingham.html (last accessed June 1, 2016).

La Rochefoucauld. *Maxims*, translated by Leonard Tancock. London: Penguin, 1959.

Lord Chesterfield. *Letters*, edited by David Roberts. New York: Cambridge University Press, 1992.

Martin, Judith. *Common Courtesy: In Which Miss Manners Solves the Problem That Baffled Mr. Jefferson*. New York: Athenaeum, 1985.

———. *Miss Manners' Guide to Rearing Perfect Children*, illustrated by Gloria Kaman. New York: Athenaeum, 1984.

———. *Miss Manners Rescues Civilization from Sexual Harassment, Frivolous Lawsuits, Dissing and Other Lapses in Civility*. New York: Crown, 1996.

————. "The World's Oldest Virtue." *First Things*, May 1993, www.firstthings.com/article/1993/05/003-the-worlds-oldest-virtue (last accessed June 1, 2016).

Mill, John Stuart. *On Liberty*, edited by David Spitz. New York: Norton, 1975.

Pascal, Blaise. *Pascal's Pensées*. New York: Dutton, 1958.

Porath, Christine, and Christine Pearson. "The Price of Incivility." *Harvard Business Review*, January–February 2013, https://hbr.org/2013/01/the-price-of-incivility/ (last accessed June 1, 2016).

Post, Peggy. *Emily Post's Etiquette*. 17th ed. New York: HarperCollins, 2004.

Post, Peggy, Anna Post, Lizzie Post, and Daniel Post Senning. *Emily Post's Etiquette: Manners for a New World*. 18th ed. New York: William Morrow, 2011.

Ronson, Jon. *So You've Been Publicly Shamed*. New York: Riverhead Books, 2015.

Runciman, David. *Political Hypocrisy: The Mask of Power, from Hobbes to Orwell and Beyond*. Princeton, NJ: Princeton University Press, 2008.

Seligman, Adam N., Robert P. Weller, Michael J. Puett, and Bennet Simon. *Ritual and Its Consequences: An Essay on the Limits of Sincerity*. New York: Oxford University Press, 2008.

Shils, Edward. *The Virtue of Civility: Selected Essays on Liberalism, Tradition, and Civil Society*, edited by Steven Grosby. Indianapolis: Liberty Fund, 1997.

Shklar, Judith N. *American Citizenship: The Quest for Inclusion*. Cambridge, MA: Harvard University, 1991.

———. *Ordinary Vices*. Cambridge, MA: Belknap Press of Harvard University Press, 1984.

Trollope, Fanny. *The Domestic Manners of Americans*, edited by Richard Mullen. New York: Oxford University Press, 1984, originally published 1832.

Truss, Lynne. *Talk to the Hand: The Utter Bloody Rudeness of the World Today, or Six Good Reasons to Stay Home and Bolt the Door*. New York: Gotham Books, 2005.

Washington, George. *Rules of Civility & Decent Behavior in Company & Conversation*. www.foundationsmag.com/civility.html (last accessed June 1, 2016).

Wilde, Oscar. "The Decay of Lying." In *Intentions*, 1–55. New York: Brentano, 1905.

Wood, Gordon S. "Interests and Disinterestedness in the Making of the Constitution." In *The Idea of America: Reflections on the Birth of the United States*, 127–69. New York: Penguin Press, 2011.

CASES

Abrams v. United States, 250 U.S. 616 (1919).
New York Times v. Sullivan, 376 U.S. 254 (1964).
Whitney v. California, 274 U.S. 357 (1927).

ACKNOWLEDGMENTS

The idea for this book first arose in conversation with my editor at Stanford University Press, Michelle Lipinski. Michelle enthusiastically supported the project from the start, and she gave me expert guidance and excellent feedback throughout the entire process. It has been a genuine pleasure to work with Michelle and the team at SUP. I also thank Jeffrey Wyneken for his fine copyediting of the manuscript.

I presented a very early version of my arguments in a workshop organized by Nina Kohn at the Syracuse University College of Law. I thank my law school colleagues for their responses and advice. At various stages in my writing, I had productive conversations about the project with Elizabeth Cohen, Glyn Morgan, and Sarah Pralle. Hannah Arterian, Lauryn Gouldin, Steve Pierson, and Nicole Watson each read complete drafts of the manuscript, and they all provided detailed and very helpful comments. I also benefited from outstanding reader reports written by Michael McCann and Susan Silbey. Michael and Susan are both absolutely first-rate interdisciplinary scholars, and their insightful suggestions improved the manuscript in many ways.

Finally, I thank my family. My parents, Roger and Vee, gave me a strong work ethic. My siblings, Bruce, Greg, and Lisa, have reminded me to not take work too seriously. I am grateful for both sides of the balance. My children, Evan and Ava, are a wonder and a delight. My wife, Jennifer, is my guiding star. This is my fourth book, and Jennifer has been with me since the first volume rolled off the presses. I have relied on her sharp mind, great tenacity, and perceptive judgment at every step along the way.

K.J.B.
Fayetteville, New York